# Jesus has a Body

written and illustrated by Jayne Ann Osborne

For my mother, who taught me to
seek the Lord early and always

MERRY ROBIN
PUBLISHING

Copyright © 2025 Jayne Ann Osborne
Artwork was hand-painted using watercolor paint, colored pencil and graphite.
Edited by Holly Boud Kolb
Typesetting by Merry Robin Publishing

Library of Congress Control Number: 2025902771

All rights reserved. No part of this book, its text or illustrations may be reproduced or transmitted in any form or by any means, electronic or mechanical, without written permission from the copyright owner. Stay honest, friends!

For information about bulk purchases, wholesale, or author visits,
please contact Jayne Ann Osborne at MerryRobinPublishing@gmail.com,
on Instagram @MerryRobinPublishing,
or visit www.MerryRobinPublishing.com.

ISBN: 978 1 962975 04 9 (paperback)
ISBN: 978 1 962975 05 6 (hardcover)

Jesus has two eyes.

Jesus has a nose.

Jesus has ten toes.

Jesus gives a gift,
not just mortal birth.

Because of Him we'll live again,
               after our time on Earth.

He showed us
how to love.

John 5:2-9

He showed us
how to pray.

Mark 6:38-46

He showed us how to listen,
John 5:2–9

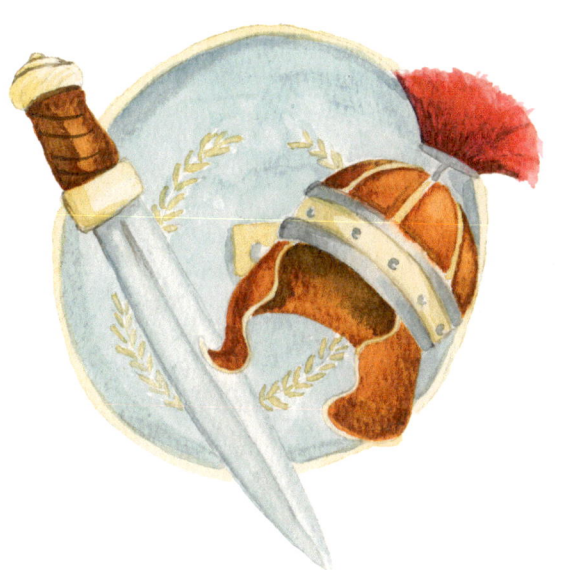

to serve,
Matthew 5:41

and to obey.
Matthew 3:13–17

Jesus has two knees.

He bent them down for me.

He folded His arms to pray

in Gethsemane.

He used His lips
to whisper

an almost silent plea,

taking upon
His shoulders

my every
pain and grief.

He helps me right my wrongs.

He invites me to repent.

And when I do, I show what His sacrifice has meant.

Jesus helps and guides me,
loves and leads the way.

Him I'll choose to follow
each and every day.

Jesus has a body,

as real as real can be,

and I can feel His love each day

as I seek Him faithfully.

# What can you do to seek Jesus today?

Find Him in the scriptures

Pray

Learn about Him in church

Think about Him

Draw a picture of Him

Ask questions

Spend time watching the sky

Sing a song about Jesus

Imagine what He looks like

Listen to stories of Jesus

Serve someone

Be kind

Take a nature walk

Listen quietly for the Spirit to whisper to your heart

## What other ideas do you have?

"Seek, and ye shall find."

## Our Literary Collection

If you enjoyed this book, you'll love our other titles!

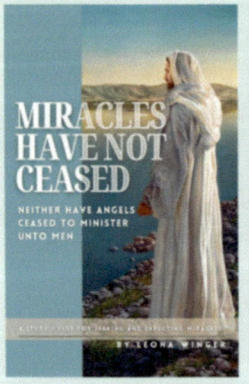
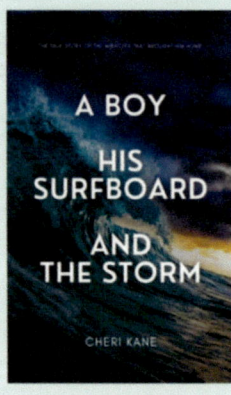

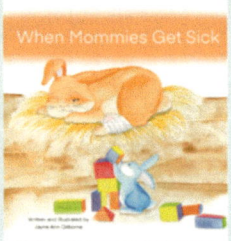

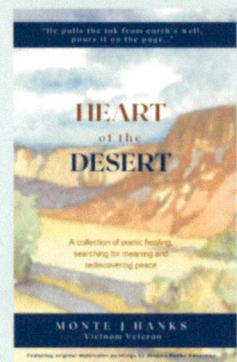
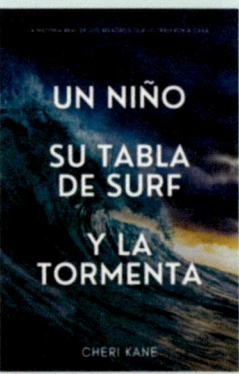

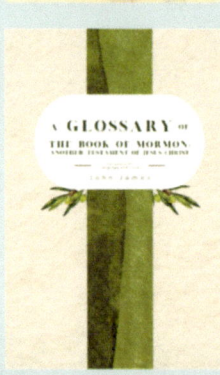

**MERRY ROBIN PUBLISHING**

MerryRobinPublishing.com

Books | Editing | Coaching | Design

Made in the USA
Columbia, SC
28 February 2025